The Bill of Rights

CHRISTINE TAYLOR-BUTLER

Children's Press®
An Imprint of Scholastic Inc.
New York Toronto London Auckland Sydney
Mexico City New Delhi Hong Kong
Danbury, Connecticut

Content Consultant

David R. Smith, PhD

Academic Adviser and

Adjunct Assistant Professor of History

University of Michigan-Ann Arbor

Reading Consultant

Cecilia Minden-Cupp, PhD

Early Literacy Consultant and Author

Library of Congress Cataloging-in-Publication Data

Taylor-Butler, Christine.
 The Bill of Rights / by Christine Taylor-Butler.
    p. cm.—(A true book)
 Includes bibliographical references and index.
 ISBN-13: 978-0-531-12627-1 (lib. bdg.)   978-0-531-14777-1 (pbk.)
 ISBN-10: 0-531-12627-7 (lib. bdg.)   0-531-14777-0 (pbk.)
 1. United States. Constitution. 1st–10th Amendments—History—Juvenile literature.
 2. Civil rights—United States—History—Juvenile literature. 3. United States.
 Constitution. 1st–10th Amendments. 4. Constitutional amendments—United States.
 5. Civil rights—United States. I. Title. II. Series.
 KF4750.T39 2008
 342.7308'5—dc22   2007012252

All rights reserved. Published in 2008 by Children's Press, an imprint of Scholastic Inc.
Published simultaneously in Canada. Printed in China. 62
SCHOLASTIC, CHILDREN'S PRESS, A TRUE BOOK, and associated logos are trademarks and/or registered trademarks of Scholastic Inc.
7 8 9 10 R 17 16 15 14 13 12 11

Find the Truth!

Everything you are about to read is true *except* for one of the sentences on this page.

Which one is **TRUE**?

T or F   The Bill of Rights was written by Thomas Jefferson.

T or F   The Bill of Rights is part of the U.S. Constitution.

Find the answer in this book.

Contents

THE **BIG** TRUTH!

Virginia passed its bill of rights 15 years before the United States did!

THE VIRGINIA DECLARATION OF RIGHTS

4 Rights for the People

What's in the Bill of Rights, and why should we care about it? **30**

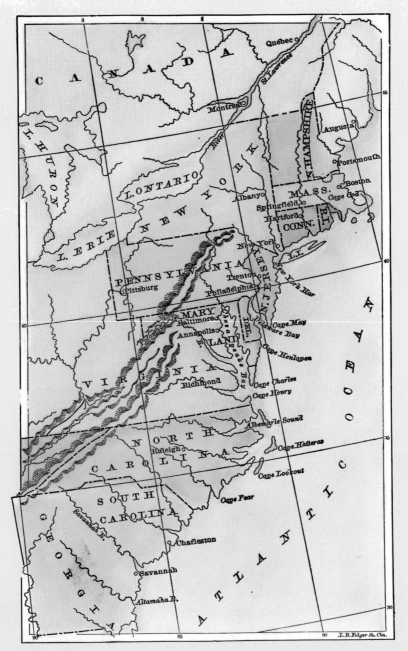

This map shows what the United States looked like around 1790.
There were only 13 states. Before becoming states, though, they were
the original 13 colonies.

CHAPTER 1

It's All About Rights

These three states approved the Bill of Rights almost 150 years after the other states!

Mass.

Conn.

Georgia

What is in the United States' Bill of Rights? Why was the idea of **rights** so important to Americans? To answer these questions, you need to know the story of how the United States became a country.

The land that is now the United States was first settled by groups of Native Americans. Thousands of years later, explorers from Europe arrived. They began claiming the land as their own.

Settlers from Great Britain established 13 **colonies**. These colonies were along the eastern coast of what is now the United States. The people who lived in the colonies were called colonists.

In this painting, colonists meet the Nauset people. These Native Americans grew corn and beans in what is now Massachusetts.

This painting shows Pilgrims leaving Plymouth, England, for their voyage to America. Of 102 settlers, nearly half died in their first winter in America.

Many colonists came to start a new life. Some hoped to become rich. Other colonists came for religious freedom. At the time, people in Great Britain could be punished for having a different religion than the rest of the country and its king.

Rights in Great Britain

With the exception of religion, the English colonists had individual rights when they lived in Great Britain. They had won rights long before, in the year 1215. Why were those rights so important?

Before 1215, British kings and queens could take people's land. They could also make them pay enormous taxes. They could even have people killed for no reason.

King John did all of those things. But in 1215, powerful landowners forced the king to sign a document called the Magna Carta (MAG-nuh Kar-tuh).

This document said the king could no longer do whatever he wanted. He now needed permission from a council (which later became Parliament). The Magna Carta also gave people the right not to be imprisoned unlawfully.

The rights of the English people kept growing. In 1689, Parliament convinced their king and queen to sign a bill of rights. This gave Parliament even more power to protect people's rights. The king and queen could no longer ignore Parliament's laws.

This image shows King John signing the Magna Carta in 1215. He did not plan to follow the document. In 1216, King John died in a civil war. His son, Henry III, was forced to follow the laws in 1225.

Rights in the United States

The colonists believed they should have the same rights as people living in Britain. But they had no voice in the British government. They had no say in how taxes were imposed. So the colonists refused to pay the taxes that the British government demanded.

To punish the colonists, the king and Parliament took away some of their rights. Parliament forced colonists to house British soldiers and closed Boston's port. The more the colonists protested, the stricter the British government became.

Even playing cards were taxed by the British!

Colonists organized to oppose the Stamp Act in 1765. This British tax required colonists to buy a stamp for all printed materials.

General George Washington was an important leader during the Revolutionary War. In this illustration, Washington leads his army at the Battle of Princeton in 1777. The Americans won the war in 1783.

The colonists decided to fight for their rights! They went to war with Great Britain in 1775. They declared their independence the next year.

But now the Americans had no central government of their own. They had always been ruled by Britain. How would they run their new country?

This engraving shows Philadelphia's Independence Hall as it was in 1776. Leaders met here to write the Bill of Rights. The Declaration of Independence and the Constitution were also signed here.

CHAPTER 2

Running the United States

On a $100 bill, Independence Hall's clock reads 4:10.

The summer of 1787 was unbearably hot in Philadelphia. Flies and mosquitoes filled the air. The smells of sweat and animal waste wafted through the streets. Despite the heat, the new nation's leading men called a meeting. They would not be stopped from planning a new government.

One Failed Attempt

The meeting called the Constitutional Convention began in May 1787. Each state, except Rhode Island, sent **delegates**, or representatives, to the convention. There were 55 delegates in attendance.

The delegates wanted to create a **constitution**. This document would outline the laws and government of the new country. These delegates are known today as the founders of the United States. Many were already famous. George

Washington had led the army against Britain in the fight for independence. Benjamin Franklin was an inventor and political leader.

This painting shows delegates at the Constitutional Convention, including George Washington (holding his hat) and Benjamin Franklin (in the brown suit, holding a cane).

James Madison's portrait is on the $5,000 bill, which is no longer printed.

Some delegates were not as well known. James Madison was an intelligent young man. Madison had helped write Virginia's constitution. He had spent many hours thinking about the new country. He studied the governments of ancient Greece and Rome. Madison filled notebooks with his thoughts. Eager to get started, he arrived in Philadelphia well prepared.

A New Constitution at Last!

The delegates worked on the new constitution for four months. They decided to keep their meetings secret. They sealed the meeting room's windows shut and posted guards. Imagine how hot it was inside!

In this painting, George Washington addresses delegates at the Constitutional Convention. There, leaders created the kind of government that still leads the United States today.

During that time, the delegates had many arguments. They were able to come to agreement on most issues. But the question of individual rights remained unsettled.

Five days before the end of the Constitutional Convention, George Mason of Virginia asked to change, or **amend**, the new constitution. He wanted Americans to have individual rights. Those rights included free speech and freedom of religion. Mason asked for a separate bill of rights.

Some delegates agreed with Mason, but most were impatient to finish. The group voted "no" to George Mason's suggestion.

The Constitution was approved on September 15, 1787. It did not have a bill of rights. Mason and two other delegates were so angry they refused to sign it. The constitution described the parts and duties of the government. It also contained rules for elections. The constitution clearly defined the role of the **federal** government.

Thirty-nine delegates signed the U.S. Constitution in 1787. You can see 22 signatures here.

The Most Modern City

In 1787, Philadelphia was the most modern city in the United States. "Modern" then was very different from today. People threw their trash into the streets. There were no toilets, only outhouses with holes in the ground. Cows, chickens, and pigs lived side by side with people. There was no air-conditioning. If you were hot, you stayed that way until the weather changed.

Why did the Constitutional Convention meet in Philadelphia? There were enough taverns, restaurants, and rooming houses to serve the large number of people traveling to the convention. Above all, the city was a symbol of hope for the new nation. It was where independence had been declared in 1776.

This oil painting shows the signing of the Constitution in 1787. At that time, the Constitution did not include a bill of rights.

Howard Chandler

CHAPTER 3

It's Not Finished Yet!

The United States has the oldest, and shortest, written constitution in the world.

You may be familiar with the first words of the U.S. Constitution. "We the People of the United States . . ." Those words show that the new government was for the good of the people. But it did not include any rights for them.

For and Against

In order for the new constitution to become law, three-quarters of the states would have to approve it. Many did not want a constitution without a bill of rights.

People who supported the Constitution called themselves Federalists. Those who did not were called Anti-Federalists. Anti-Federalists tried to convince their states to vote against approving the Constitution. They wanted a formal bill of rights.

Federalists and Anti-Federalists do battle in this cartoon.

vi CONTENTS.

THE

THE
FEDERALIST:
ADDRESSED TO THE
PEOPLE OF THE STATE OF NEW-YORK.

NUMBER I.

Introduction.

AFTER an unequivocal experience of the inefficacy of the ſubſiſting federal government, you are called upon to deliberate on a new conſtitution for the United States of America. The ſubject ſpeaks its own importance; comprehending in its conſequences, nothing leſs than the exiſtence of the UNION, the ſafety and welfare of the parts of which it is compoſed, the fate of an empire, in many reſpects, the moſt intereſting in the world. It has been frequently remarked, that it ſeems to have been reſerved to the people of this country, by their conduct and example, to decide the important queſtion, whether ſocieties of men are really capable or not, of eſtabliſhing good government from reflection and choice, or whether they are forever deſtined to depend, for their political conſtitutions, on accident and force. If there be any truth in the remark, the criſis, at which we are arrived, may with propriety be regarded as the æra in which
A   that

James Madison and other important leaders wrote 85 essays in support of the Constitution. These essays are called *The Federalist Papers.*

Many states had their own constitutions and bills of rights. Virginia's bill of rights passed in 1776.

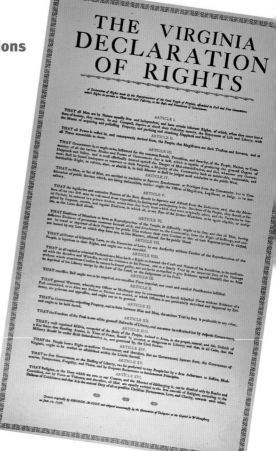

George Mason urged Virginia not to vote in favor of the Constitution. He wrote out suggestions for a bill of rights for the country. Thomas Jefferson called him "the wisest man of his generation."

Federalists had a few reasons for not wanting a bill of rights. Many states' constitutions already included bills of rights. Wasn't that enough? Some argued that it was impossible to include everything in a bill of rights. They feared that people would think the written rights were their *only* rights.

Disagreement

The arguments continued for two years. The Constitution was finally approved. However, many of the states still wanted to add a bill of rights. They began proposing changes, or **amendments**. There were more than 120 **proposals**! Those proposals were the starting point for what would become the final bill of rights.

In 1789, George Washington made the first presidential Thanksgiving Proclamation to give thanks for the Constitution.

This illustration shows George Washington being inaugurated as the first president of the United States, on April 30, 1789.

1916

Let the people vote on all acts of war; anyone voting yes has to register as an army volunteer.

1971

Have the right to an environment free of pollution.

1933

Outlaw any citizen from being worth more than $1 million.

2005

Get rid of taxes.

Trying to Change

Out of more than 11,000 requests to amend the Constitution, only 27 ever made it. One reason for this: It's hard to get an amendment approved by both Congress and the state governments. Another reason: Some proposals are really strange. Here are a few that didn't make it.

1810
Outlaw U.S. citizens from becoming royalty in another country.

1878
Replace the president with a three-person council.

1893
Change the country's name to "United States of Earth."

CHAPTER **4**

Rights for the People

On December 15, 1791, Virginia's approval met the 3/4 requirement and ratified the Bill of Rights.

The states proposed 200 amendments to the Constitution. But that was too many for a bill of rights. The list needed to be shortened. James Madison took the lead in deciding what was most important.

James Madison held several government offices before he was elected to be the fourth president in 1808.

James Madison

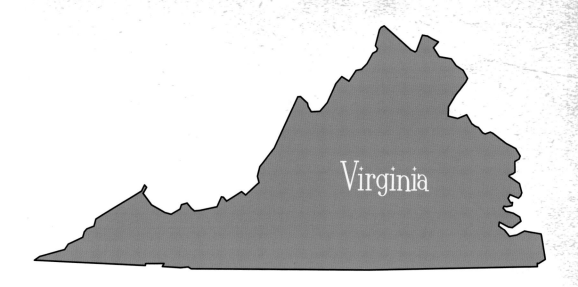

Virginia

Madison suggested several amendments. From these, Congress reduced the list to 12 amendments and sent them to the states. For the amendments to pass, nine states needed to vote in favor of them.

Ten of the 12 amendments were approved by the states. Those 10 amendments became the original U.S. Bill of Rights.

The Bill of Rights promises to protect and maintain certain rights and freedoms for U.S. **citizens**. Which rights and freedoms are included?

The First Amendment gives Americans the right to choose any religion, or no religion.

The First Amendment Freedoms

The First Amendment guarantees freedoms of religion, speech, and the press. It also gives people the rights to assemble peacefully and to complain directly to the government.

The Fight for Rights

1776
The American colonies declare independence from Britain.

1787
The Constitution is written.

In 1965, Martin Luther King Jr. leads a march for equal rights for African Americans. The First Amendment protected his right to speak out.

Martin Luther King Jr.

What does this mean? It means you have the right to worship in any way you wish. Freedom of speech and of the press means that you can say or write your opinion. This amendment also protects your right to meet with other people for any reason. You have the right to tell elected officials what you like and don't like.

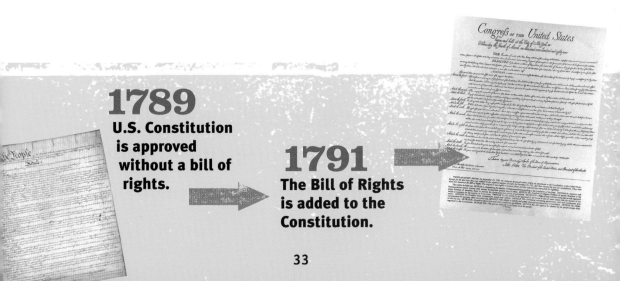

1789
U.S. Constitution is approved without a bill of rights.

1791
The Bill of Rights is added to the Constitution.

Congress of the United States

At the time the Second Amendment was passed, people used guns to hunt for food and defend their families.

The Second Amendment

This amendment states that people have the right to bear arms, or weapons, to establish a **militia.** What does this mean? People disagree over this issue. Some believe this amendment gives individuals the right to own guns. Others believe it grants states the right to defend themselves.

The Third and Fourth Amendments

American colonists once had to let British soldiers stay in their homes. The Third Amendment says no one has to house a soldier in times of peace.

The Fourth Amendment says that the government may not search citizens' homes or take their property without a reason. This means that the government or police need a judge's permission to search somebody's house.

This police officer may not search this home without special permission.

The Fifth Amendment

The Fifth Amendment gives many important rights to citizens accused of a crime. It says that a person is innocent until proven guilty. No person can be tried for the same crime twice. No property can be taken by the government without payment.

You may also have heard of people "taking the fifth." Sometimes, people are forced to testify in court. For some people, telling the truth might force them to say something that could get them arrested. The fifth amendment allows these people to refuse to testify.

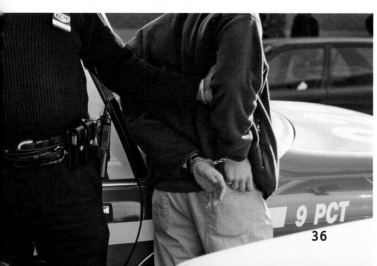

Any American accused of a crime is protected by the Fifth Amendment.

Amendments Related to Trials

The Sixth, Seventh, and Eighth Amendments list rights related to trials. A person has the right to a speedy trial, with a jury. A **jury** is a group of citizens chosen to rule on evidence in a trial.

People have the right to have a lawyer. A court cannot force people to pay fines that are too large for the crime.

These amendments help innocent people to avoid going to jail. They also ensure that guilty people are not punished too harshly.

People accused of crimes can choose to have either a jury or a judge rule on their cases.

The Ninth and Tenth Amendments

The Ninth Amendment states that the rights in the Constitution are not the only rights available to people. This means that Americans have more rights than those stated in the Bill of Rights.

The Tenth Amendment states that the federal government gets *only* the rights that the Constitution gives it. All other rights belong to the states or to the people.

Who Was Left Out?

The Bill of Rights was created to protect the rights of American citizens. There was just one problem. Women, African Americans, and Native Americans

Carol Moseley Braun was the first African-American woman elected to the U.S. Senate. She was elected in 1993.

were not considered citizens with rights under the law. They could not vote. They could not serve in government. The Constitution and the Bill of Rights were for white men. Many years later, amendments were passed that ensured rights for all citizens.

In 1941, President Franklin D. Roosevelt declared December 15 as Bill of Rights Day.

Why Should We Care?

Do you like to read comic books? Magazines? Mystery novels? You can read almost anything you want in the United States because of the Bill of Rights. Some countries have laws that prevent their citizens from reading books the government doesn't like. This is called **censorship**.

In some countries, people cannot choose their own religion. The Bill of Rights says you are free to follow any religion you like. You can choose not to worship at all. The Bill of Rights also protects your right to privacy. No one, not even a principal or teacher, can search your things without having a good reason.

As long as your parents approve, you can read almost anything you want in the United States.

40

Get Out the Vote!

In 1870, the 15th Amendment granted the right to vote to any citizen regardless of race or color. However, "citizen" still only meant "men." As of 1900, women in only a handful of western territories and states had the right to vote.

Things changed in 1920. That year, the 19th Amendment granted the right to vote to any citizen, man or woman. Finally, all American women were allowed to vote.

The work that the founders started 200 years ago protects people of every race and religion. It promises that U.S. citizens will remain free. That includes you! ★

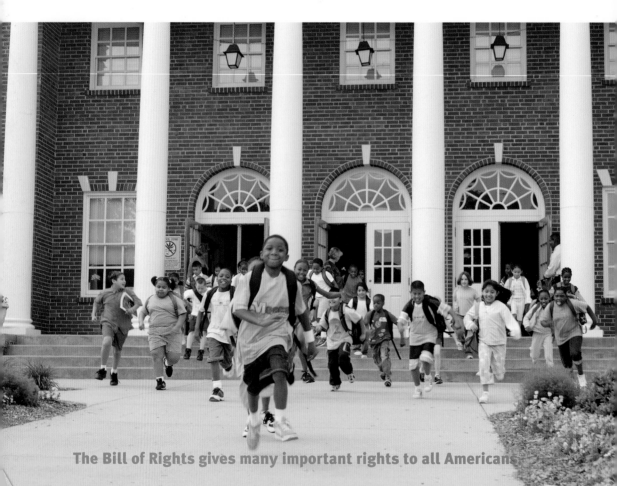

The Bill of Rights gives many important rights to all Americans.

True Statistics

Number of amendments in the original Bill of Rights: 10

Written in: 1789

Drafted by: James Madison

First state to vote for the Bill of Rights: New Jersey, on November 20, 1789

Percentage of states needed to pass: 75

Number of the original 13 colonies that approved the Bill of Rights by 1791: 10

State that made the Bill of Rights effective: Virginia, on December 15, 1791

On display today at: National Archives in Washington, D.C.

Delivered to the National Archives in: 1952

Did you find the truth?

F The Bill of Rights was written by Thomas Jefferson.

T The Bill of Rights is part of the U.S. Constitution.

Resources

Books

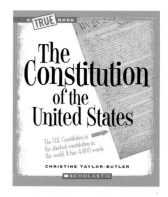

Burgan, Michael. *The Bill of Rights*. Minneapolis: Compass Point Books, 2002.

Freedman, Russell. *In Defense of Liberty: The Story of America's Bill of Rights*. New York: Holiday House, 2003.

Krull, Kathleen. *A Kids' Guide to America's Bill of Rights*. New York: Avon Books, 1999.

Landau, Elaine. *Women's Right to Vote*. Danbury, CT: Children's Press, 2005.

Marcovitz, Hal. *The Constitution*. Philadelphia: Mason Crest Publishers, 2003.

Taylor-Butler, Christine. *The Constitution*. Danbury, CT: Children's Press, 2008.

Venezia, Mike. *James Madison*. Danbury, CT: Children's Press, 2004.

Yero, Judith Lloyd. *The Bill of Rights*. Washington, DC: National Geographic Children's Books, 2006.

Organizations and Web Sites

Bill of Rights Institute
www.billofrightsinstitute.org
Look for "eLessons" about the Bill of Rights and the founders.

The Constitution for Kids
www.usConstitution.net/constkids4.html
Check out this Web site for kids, grades four to seven.

Independence Hall Association
www.ushistory.org
Find numerous links to people, sites, and events in history.

White House
www.whitehouse.gov/kids/constitution/billofrights.html
Find the exact wording of the Bill of Rights, as well as links.

Places to Visit

National Archives
700 Pennsylvania Avenue NW
Washington, DC 20408-0001
202-357-5000
www.archives.gov
Visit the Bill of Rights, see letters from George Washington, and more.

National Constitution Center
525 Arch Street
Independence Mall
Philadelphia, PA 19106
215-409-6600
www.constitutioncenter.org
Why is the Constitution important to you? Visit this center for the answer.

Important Words

amend – to change or add to a legal document or law

amendment – change or addition to a legal document or law

censorship – government restrictions on a book, film, or other form of expression that is considered harmful or improper according to certain standards

colonies – lands settled and ruled by people from another country on behalf of the government of their country

constitution (kon-stuh-TOO-shun) – a document that describes the basic laws and organization of a government

delegates – people chosen to represent others at a meeting

federal – relating to a form of government in which states are united under one central power

jury – a group of citizens chosen to listen to and rule on evidence in a trial

militia (muh-LI-shuh) – a group of civilians trained as soldiers, who serve only in emergencies

proposals – suggestions, such as laws or plans, that others can consider approving or rejecting

rights – people's freedoms, as guaranteed by law

Index

About the Author

Christine Taylor-Butler has written more than 30 books for children. She has written several books in the True Book American History series, including *The Constitution*, *The Congress of the United States*, *The Supreme Court*, and *The Presidency*.

A native of Ohio, Taylor-Butler now lives in Kansas City, Missouri, with her husband, Ken, and their two daughters. She holds degrees in both civil engineering and art and design from the Massachusetts Institute of Technology.